et Crafty Outdoors

Science and Craft Proje

WEATHER

by Ruth Owen

PowerKiDS press.

New York

Published in 2013 by The Rosen Publishing Group, Inc.
29 East 21st Street, New York, NY 10010

Produced for Rosen by Ruby Tuesday Books Ltd
Editor for Ruby Tuesday Books Ltd: Mark J. Sachner
US Editor: Sara Antill
Designer: Emma Randall

Photo Credits:
Cover, 1, 4–5, 6–7, 10–11, 12–13, 14–15, 16–17, 18–19, 22, 23 (top), 24, 25 (top right), 26–27 © Shutterstock; 8–9, 20–21, 25 (top left), 25 (bottom), 28–29 © Ruby Tuesday Books Ltd; 23 (bottom) © National Weather Service, Aberdeen, South Dakota.

Publisher Cataloging Data

Owen, Ruth, 1967–
        Science and craft projects with weather / by Ruth Owen.
p.   cm. — (Get crafty outdoors)
Includes index.
Summary: This book defines weather, tells what makes different types of weather happen, and provides instructions to make weather-related craft projects.
Contents: Weather watching — What's the temperature? — Make a sun catcher — The water cycle — Water cycle friendship bracelets — Wet weather — Make a rainy day collage — Snowy weather — Paper snowflakes — Hailstones — Make icy garden stones — Thunder and lightning — Make a weather wheel.
        ISBN 978-1-4777-0244-4 (library binding) — ISBN 978-1-4777-0251-2 (pbk.) — ISBN 978-1-4777-0252-9 (6-pack)
        1. Weather—Juvenile literature   2. Meteorology—Juvenile literature   3. Handicraft—Juvenile literature   (1. Weather   2. Meteorology   3. Handicraft)
I. Title
                2013
        551.5—dc23

Manufactured in the United States of America

CPSIA Compliance Information: Batch #W13PK7: For Further Information contact Rosen Publishing, New York, New York at 1-800-237-9932

Contents

Weather Watching

Why is it that sometimes we wear shorts and sunglasses outside, but at other times we need to wear a coat, a scarf, and gloves? The answer is weather! Sunshine, rain, snow, and thunderstorms are all types of weather.

Weather can be very different from place to place, even at the same time of year. In winter there may be lots of snow in Chicago. A winter day in Florida, however, may be so warm and sunny that people visit the beach.

a snowy day

Windy Weather

Wind is a type of weather that happens when air moves around. You can't see the wind, but when it blows your hair around your face or nearly pushes you over, you know it's there!

a windy day

This book is all about the weather. You will find out what makes different types of weather happen. You will also get the chance to make some neat weather crafts!

What's the Temperature?

One important part of weather is how hot or cold the temperature is outside.

To measure the temperature, we use units of measurement called **degrees**. Instead of writing the word degrees, we can use a **symbol** that looks like a tiny circle: °.

You can find out the temperature by looking at a thermometer. The red **liquid** inside the thermometer goes up as the temperature gets hotter and down as the temperature cools. The top of the red line shows how many degrees the temperature is against a scale.

A bathing suit, sunglasses, and sunscreen are just right for a hot, sunny day.

thermometer

There are two different temperature scales. One is called the Fahrenheit scale. The other is the Celsius scale. Some people use Fahrenheit temperatures, and others use Celsius. Most thermometers show both scales.

Celsius temperature scale

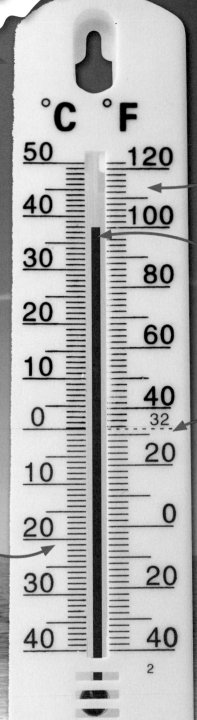

Fahrenheit temperature scale

very hot temperature

freezing cold temperature

Reading a Thermometer

This thermometer is showing a very hot temperature of 100 degrees Fahrenheit, or 100°F. This is the same as 38 degrees Celsius, or 38°C. When the temperature drops to 32°F and 0°C, the weather is so cold that the water on top of a pond will freeze.

Make a Sun Catcher

It's great to look out of the window and see that the weather is sunny. Make this colorful Sun catcher, and you will have Sun in your window every day!

You will need:

- Yellow, orange, and red finger paint
- 3 flat dishes or containers
- White construction paper
- Scissors
- A piece of cardboard at least 8 inches by 8 inches (20 x 20 cm)
- A ruler
- A paintbrush
- Glue
- Wax paper
- Yellow, orange, and red wax crayons
- A cheese grater
- A small bowl
- An iron
- Cotton or ribbon
- An adult to be your teammate

Get Crafty:

1 Ask an adult to help you pour the paint into flat containers or dishes.

2 On the construction paper make up to 10 paint handprints in yellow, orange, and red. Then ask an adult to help you cut out the handprints.

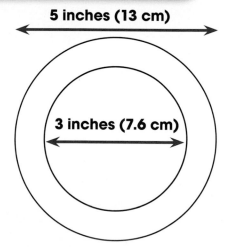

5 inches (13 cm)

3 inches (7.6 cm)

3 Ask an adult to cut a doughnut shape from the cardboard. It should measure about 5 inches (13 cm) across. The inner circle should measure about 3 inches (7.6 cm) across.

4 Paint the doughnut shape yellow. Glue the handprints to the back of the doughnut shape to make the Sun.

5 Ask an adult to cut two circles of wax paper that are 4 inches (10 cm) across.

6 Grate the crayons into a small bowl being very careful not to rub your fingers against the grater. Mix up the different-colored pieces of crayon in the bowl.

7 Sprinkle some grated crayon onto one of the wax paper circles. Then place the other wax paper circle on top, so you have a crayon sandwich.

8 Now ask an adult to iron the wax paper crayon sandwich using a cool iron. Keep ironing until the crayons melt and swirl together.

9 Finally, glue the crayon sandwich to the back of your Sun.

10 Hang your Sun catcher in a sunny window. When light shines through the center of the Sun, it will make colors in the room!

The Water Cycle

When it's pouring rain outside, have you ever wondered how all that water got up into the sky? It's because of a process called the **water cycle**.

Warmth from the Sun turns water from ponds, rivers, the ocean, and even puddles into a **gas** called **water vapor**.

Water Vapor

Water on Earth is changing into water vapor all day, every day. It's not possible to see water vapor, but it is in the air all around us!

This puddle is getting smaller as the water becomes vapor.

The water vapor rises up high into the sky. Many miles (km) above Earth, the air is extremely cold. The cold air turns the vapor back into tiny drops of water.

The water drops stick to bits of dust in the air. Billions of tiny water drops join together to make clouds.

clouds

Inside a cloud, the water drops get bigger and heavier, until finally they fall back to Earth as rain. The water cycle is complete.

Water Cycle Friendship Bracelets

Here's a fantastic way to help you remember how the water cycle works. You can make colorful friendship bracelets that show the water cycle's different stages.

You will need:

- Yellow, clear, white, blue, and green beads
- Leather cord or elastic thread
- Scissors

Get Crafty:

1 You can buy beads from bead shops, craft stores, and online. You can also ask the adults you know if they have any strings of beads or jewelry they no longer want so that you can recycle the beads.

2 Here is what the differently colored beads will stand for in your bracelet.

yellow beads = the Sun

clear beads = water vapor

white beads = clouds

blue beads = rain

elastic thread

green beads = Earth

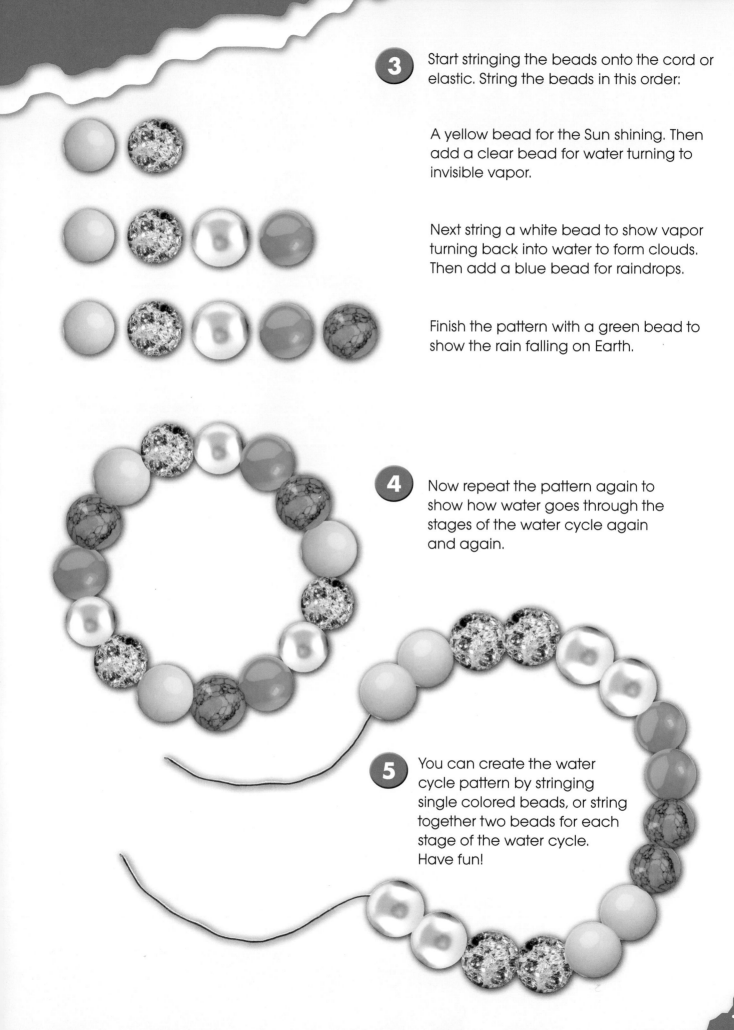

3 Start stringing the beads onto the cord or elastic. String the beads in this order:

A yellow bead for the Sun shining. Then add a clear bead for water turning to invisible vapor.

Next string a white bead to show vapor turning back into water to form clouds. Then add a blue bead for raindrops.

Finish the pattern with a green bead to show the rain falling on Earth.

4 Now repeat the pattern again to show how water goes through the stages of the water cycle again and again.

5 You can create the water cycle pattern by stringing single colored beads, or string together two beads for each stage of the water cycle. Have fun!

Wet Weather

Each raindrop in a cloud can be made up from millions of tiny water drops. Raindrops can be as tiny as a grain of sand, or as large as the fingernail on your little finger.

When raindrops hit your umbrella, they may have come from a cloud that's floating 3 miles (4.8 km) above your head!

Rain splashes into puddles, ponds, rivers, and the ocean. Some rain falls on land, too, and soaks into the ground.

A raincoat, rubber boots, and umbrella are just right for a wet, rainy day.

Once the rainwater is back on Earth, it may go through the water cycle again within a few days or even hours. The water might stay on Earth for thousands of years, however.

A puddle is a good place for animals to take a bath!

When No Rain Falls

Sometimes no rain, or less rain than expected, falls in an area. After many months, or even years, the lack of rain causes a **drought**. Lakes and rivers dry up so people and animals do not have enough water to drink. **Crops** cannot grow without water, so people do not have enough to eat.

This corn is struggling to grow in dry ground caused by a drought.

Make a Rainy Day Collage

Using paint, colored paper, foil, cotton balls, fabric scraps, and pictures from magazines, make a collage picture of a rainy day.

You will need:

- A large sheet of construction paper
- A paintbrush
- Blue paint
- Scissors
- Glue stick
- Aluminum foil
- Cotton balls
- Colored paper, felt, and fabric scraps
- A hole punch
- Old magazines
- An adult to be your teammate and to help with cutting

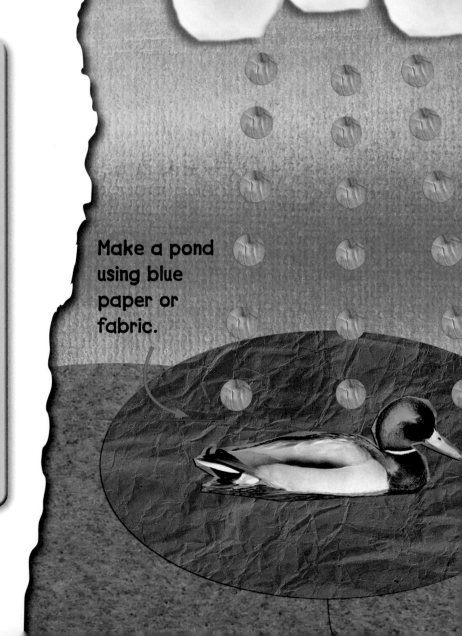

Make a pond using blue paper or fabric.

Get Crafty:

Glue cotton balls onto the sky to make fluffy clouds.

Cut photographs from old magazines.

1 Paint the sheet of paper blue to make the sky.

2 At the bottom of your picture, you can make hills using colored paper or fabric. Ask an adult to help you with any cutting.

3 Now it's time to make the rainy scene. You can make a picture like the one on this page, or get creative with your own ideas. Look at the labels on this collage picture for some ideas to get you started.

Use a hole punch to cut tiny circles of foil as raindrops.

Make puddles from foil.

Snowy Weather

Sometimes it is so cold inside a cloud that the tiny water drops freeze. Instead of forming raindrops, the drops become pieces of ice called crystals.

A snowplow clears snow from a road during a blizzard.

The ice crystals stick together and form snowflakes. No two snowflakes look the same. Every snowflake has its own pattern.

When a cloud contains snowflakes, snow falls to the ground instead of rain.

Sometimes storms called **blizzards** happen. During a blizzard, huge amounts of snow fall, and there are very strong winds.

Having a snowball fight is great fun!

Snowflake Patterns

Every snowflake has six arms that branch out from its center. A snowflake is also symmetrical through its center. This means if you draw a line through the snowflake's middle, the two halves will mirror each other.

line of symmetry

a close-up photo of a real snowflake

Paper Snowflakes

Try making these cool paper snowflakes to hang up as a winter decoration. Remember, your snowflakes must have six arms and be symmetrical.

You will need:

- Sheets of white paper
- Scissors
- Tape or glue
- Ribbon or string for hanging the snowflakes

Get Crafty:

1 Ask an adult to help you cut the paper into strips about 5 inches (13 cm) long. Cut some strips that are 1 inch (2.5 cm) wide, and some that are 0.5 inch (1.3 cm) wide.

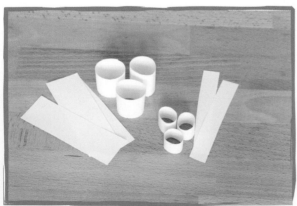

2 Roll the paper strips into circular coils and use the tape or glue to secure them. Make large coils and small coils, but remember, for your snowflake to be symmetrical you must have coils that match each other for size.

3 Now, try making snowflake shapes using the coils.
You can mix up large coils and small coils.

4 Once you have made a snowflake shape that you like, glue or tape all the coils
together. Tie a piece of ribbon or string through one of the coils at the end of an arm.
Your snowflake is ready to hang up.

5 Try making lots of different snowflakes and then hang them up together.

Hailstones

There is another type of weather that falls from clouds—hailstones!

hailstones

Hailstones form inside huge thunderstorm clouds, where it is very windy.

Inside the cloud, the wind blows water drops up high, where it is cold. The drops freeze into icy balls, or hailstones.

The hailstones then fall back down in the cloud, and more water drops stick to them. Then they are blown up high again, and this new water freezes, too.

As more water sticks to each hailstone and then freezes, the hailstone gets bigger and bigger. Finally, the hailstones fall down to Earth!

layers

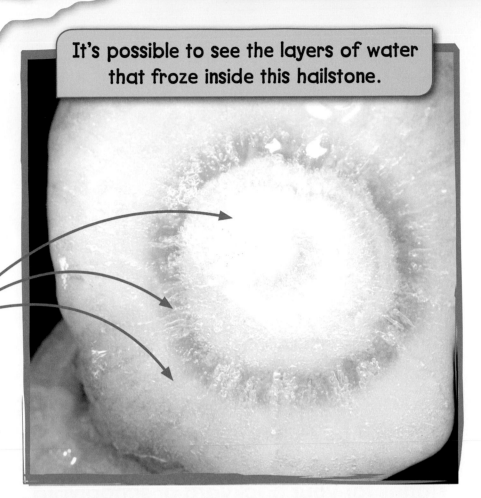

It's possible to see the layers of water that froze inside this hailstone.

Giant Hailstones

Hailstones are usually about the size of a pea. Sometimes, however, they can be the size of a marble or even a golf ball. In 2010, a hailstone that measured 8 inches (20.3 cm) fell from the sky in Vivian, South Dakota!

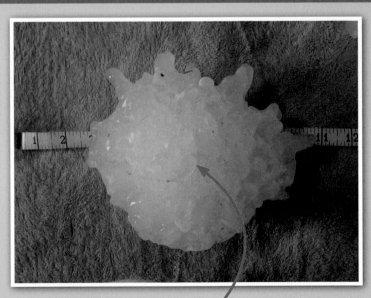

the hailstone from Vivian, South Dakota

Make Icy Garden Stones

Water is amazing stuff! When liquid water gets warm, it turns into a gas. Then, when that gas gets cool, it turns back into water. When water gets very, very cold, it freezes and becomes solid. If water didn't change in this way, we wouldn't have rain, snow, or hailstones. Here's a fun project to turn water into ice to make pretty, decorative garden stones for your backyard or schoolyard.

You will need:

- Foil dishes 6 to 8 inches (15–20 cm) across
- Water
- Food coloring in different colors
- A paintbrush
- Pretty pebbles, leaves, or flowers
- A thermometer
- Freezing cold weather or a freezer

Get Crafty:

1. If it is winter you can make this project outdoors. Put a thermometer outside and after two hours check to see if the red line is on or below 32°F (0°C), on the scale. If it is, it means the weather is cold enough to turn water into ice.

2. If you want to make this craft and the weather is not freezing cold, you can use a freezer.

3. Fill the foil dishes with water.

4. Now comes the really fun part. To make a colored garden stone, put 5 drops of food coloring into the dish. Stir the water with a paintbrush.

5 You can make clear garden stones, too. Try dropping some pebbles, leaves, or flowers into the water to add some decoration.

**dishes of water
with food coloring**

pretty pebbles

flowers

colorful leaves

6 Leave your garden stones to freeze outside. If you are making them in a freezer, put them in the freezer overnight.

7 When the water in the dishes has frozen solid, tip the garden stones out of the dishes. Now they are ready to be placed in your backyard or schoolyard.

8 In winter, the garden stones will last for as long as the temperature stays low. At other times of the year, watch to see how quickly the icy garden stones become water again.

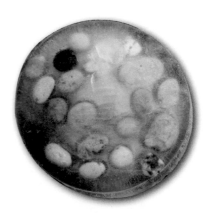

Thunder and Lightning

When you see flashes in the sky and hear thunder claps, it can only be one type of weather—a thunderstorm!

thunderstorm cloud

As a huge, dark thunderstorm cloud moves through the sky, it rubs against the air around it. This makes a type of electricity, called **static electricity**, build up in the cloud.

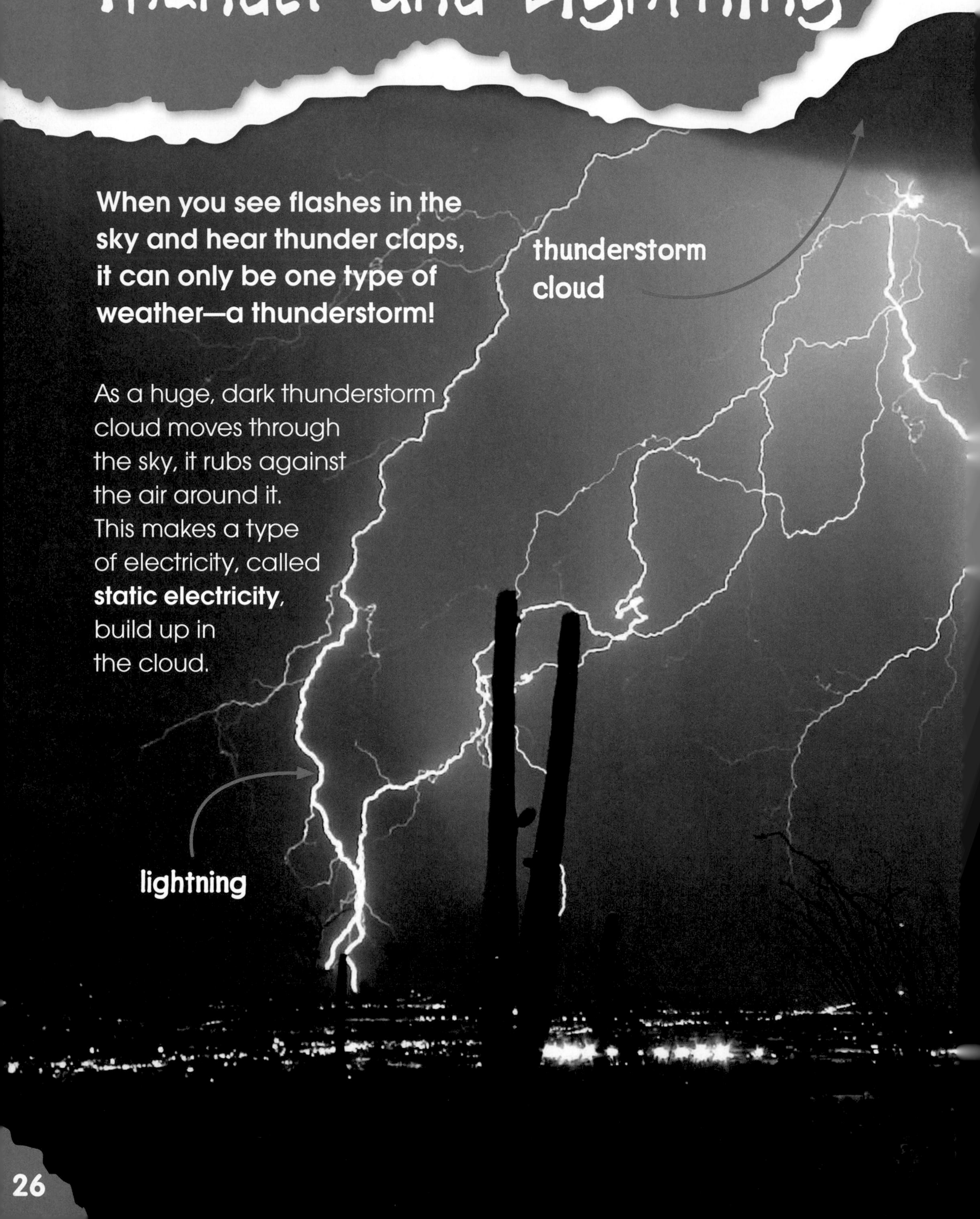

lightning

The electricity produces the flashes of lightning that we see. Lightning flashes travel at 60,000 miles per second (97,000 km/s).

A lightning flash opens up a long hole, or tunnel, in the air. When the flash has passed, the air instantly collapses back into the tunnel. This movement of air causes the rumbling, or cracking, thunder noise.

Tornadoes

Sometimes the air inside a thunderstorm cloud begins to spin faster and faster, forming a huge column. When the spinning column hits the ground, it is called a tornado. As it moves along the ground, a tornado can uproot trees and destroy buildings!

Make a Weather Wheel

What type of weather happens where you live? Make this great weather wheel, and you can turn the arrow to show what the weather is like each day!

You will need:

- A paper plate
- A pencil
- A ruler
- A black marker
- Glue

- To make our weather wheel we used paints, bubble wrap, foil, salt, and black paper
- A small piece of colorful cardboard
- A brass fastener
- An adult to be your teammate and to help with cutting

Get Crafty:

1 Make a list of the types of weather you have where you live. Choose six types of weather that happen most often.

2 Using the pencil and ruler, draw lines to divide the plate into six equal sections. Then ink in the lines with the marker.

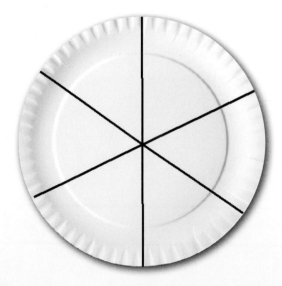

3 Now draw, paint, or glue craft materials to the plate to show the six types of weather you see most. Ask an adult to help you with any cutting. Here's what we did:

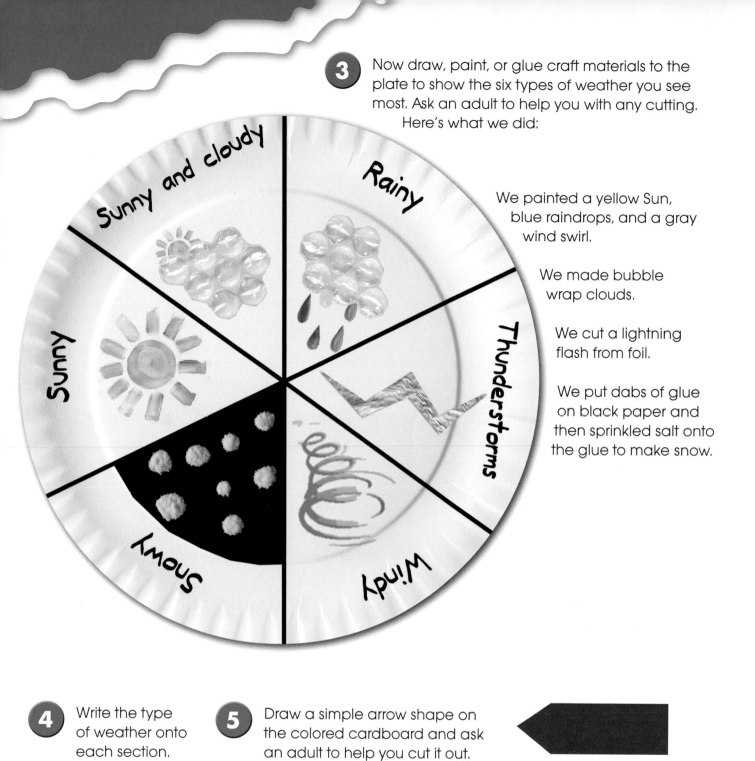

We painted a yellow Sun, blue raindrops, and a gray wind swirl.

We made bubble wrap clouds.

We cut a lightning flash from foil.

We put dabs of glue on black paper and then sprinkled salt onto the glue to make snow.

4 Write the type of weather onto each section.

5 Draw a simple arrow shape on the colored cardboard and ask an adult to help you cut it out.

6 Ask an adult to pierce a hole in the center of the plate and in the square end of the arrow. Then pin the arrow to the plate using the brass fastener.

Glossary

blizzard (BLIH-zurd)
A storm during which lots of snow falls and there are very strong winds.

crops (KRAHPS)
Plants that are grown in large quantities on a farm.

degree (dih-GREE)
A unit of measurement used to measure how hot or cold something is.

drought (DROWT)
A time when no rain, or less rain than usual, falls in an area.

gas (GAS)
Matter, such as water vapor, that is neither a solid or a liquid.

liquid (LIH-kwed)
Something that flows, such as water, and changes its shape to fit any container it is placed in.

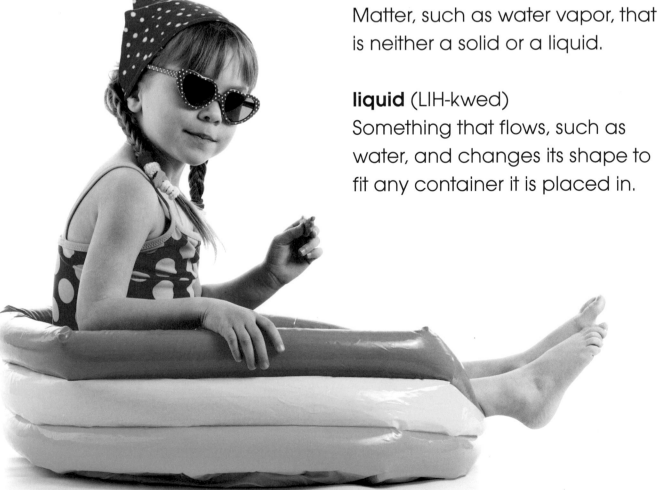

static electricity
(STA-tik ih-lek-TRIH-suh-tee)
A type of electricity that is
produced when two things
are rubbed together.

symbol (SIM-bul)
A picture that is used to stand
for something else.

water cycle (WAH-ter SY-kul)
The process in which water
moves from Earth, up into the
sky to make clouds, and back
down to Earth again.

water vapor (WAH-ter VAY-pur)
Water that has turned into a gas.

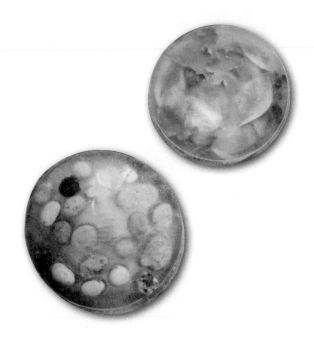

Websites

Due to the changing nature of Internet links, PowerKids Press has
developed an online list of websites related to the subject of this book.
This site is updated regularly. Please use this link to access the list:
www.powerkidslinks.com/gco/weath/

Read More

Furgang, Kathy. *Everything Weather: Facts, Photos, and Fun That Will Blow Your Mind!.* Des Moines, IA: National Geographic Children's Books, 2012.

Libbrecht, Kenneth. *The Secret Life of a Snowflake: An Up-Close Look at the Art and Science of Snowflakes.* Minneapolis, MN: Voyageur Press, 2010.

Morgan, Sally. *The Water Cycle.* Nature's Cycles. New York: PowerKids Press, 2009.

Index